Liminal Inside

LIMINAL INSIDE

a poetry collection

TW GLAES

Cunnian Press

Oregon

ISBN: 979-8-9903058-0-9

Print Font: EB Garamond

eBook ISBN: 979-8-9903058-1-6

Book Cover by T.W. Glaes (All proper rights for use and distribution obtained.)

Visual Designs by T.W. Glaes (All proper rights for use and distribution were obtained.)

First Edition Paperback: July 2024

For those who find beauty in
sadness and loneliness.

For the ones who are overlooked,
forgotten, abandoned, invisible,
unheard, and taken for granted.

This is for the misunderstood.

I hope you find solace and peaceful
reflection in these pages.

Content Warning

Read at your own risk.

These poems are the sound of my heart when it bleeds.

Some of them are the sound of personal victories.

If you do not enjoy or find beauty in sad, or potentially trig-
gering poems that end with no resolution, topics of emotional
health and exploration, or poems with dark themes, forlorn
tones, and speculative dark imagery, then this probably isn't the
book for you.

If you choose to proceed, read these poems with grace, kindness,
and humility toward yourself and toward the author.

CONTENTS

We Built a Castle

We built a castle on the apparitions of our broken dreams —

Patched the roof and walls with visions anew.

We filled the moat with shadows of our ancient wounds —

Guarded the door with

Pain's strength and fang.

In the garden, we exhumed from our endurance

a cache of yarrow, calendula, rosemary, and sage.

Resilient as ivy, we climbed toward the sun —

despite every cut from outlanders and false friends.

1

Our blood seeped into the nether —

from the red drops grew dogwood, clover, and fern.

We stocked our library with reverie and starlight,

and paved the hallways with discovery

for self-transformations beyond

society's net.

At the stone gate, we left a sign —

Only visitors with grace, health, and vision

to exchange are welcome.

Unsteady
{Yellow Tape}

I built a wall with unsteady hands,

Uneven stones, moss and mud.

I built it high, too high to climb,

Too thick to break,

Big enough to enclose a forest in wake.

Within the walls

I outlined my ruined life in chalk,

Bound my heart in yellow tape:

Crime Scene Do Not Cross.

I measured my wounds

In ounces of tea and herbs,

Let the mists set in,

And watched the thorns emerge.

I dug deep into the earth

With blood-crusted hands —

A pit for my memories,

And ragged shards of soul.

I set them ablaze —

Watched it all turn to ash.

I grasped the singed, rain-soaked ground;

A rageful prayer for life to grow back.

With heavy steps, I walked —

Iron-ice lantern in hand,

I searched for apparitions of myself

Haunting the hills of this cursed land.

A *thud* sounded near the wall,

Where ivy and ferns grow.

I thought it a shadow of self;

Another fallen piece — alone.

There, in the swirling fog and greens,

A sharp rock — chiseled from my wall.

On it, a crooked note wrapped in string

With dripping words in my own scrawl:

I miss you, Fervent Soul.

Courage, Health, Peace,

Dear Heart,

It's time you took this life apart.

Together — with my ghost I'd left outside —

Stone by stone, we made an archway; it cut my hide.

I let myself in and traded my bonds.

Yellow tape barred the arc, and marked all fronds:

Caution — Under Construction —

For All
the Times

For all the times

you got burnt

so someone else

wouldn't have to.

For all the times

you spoke out

but no one

heard you.

9

For all the times

your light began to shine,

but then it died

because they caged you.

.

For all the times

you dragged yourself

through the mud

because no one

was there to help you.

For all the times

they spilled your blood

when all your heart needed

was for them to patch you.

For all the times

you saved yourself

because no one else

would stay for you.

For all the times

you found yourself

because no one else

would claim you.

For all the times

you stood strong

when no one needed

or wanted you.

For all the times

you chose yourself

when no one else

would choose you.

For all the times

you found courage

when no one else

fought for you.

For all the times

they cast you away,

but you lived without them

despite the pain that they

never took the time to know you.

For all the times

you couldn't be yourself,

because they refused

to understand you.

For all the times

you heard yourself

when you fell silent

and withdrew.

For all the times

you fell asleep alone,

with only the sound and light

from your favorite show

to comfort you.

For all the times

one person carried it all

and that person — was you.

This time —

you are not invisible here.

Kenós

The streets have turned to oceans

Oceans of silence —

and suspended sorrow.

Faint leaves —

The crisp scrape

stumbles across the cold,

dry cement

where steps and laughter

once thrived —

now ghosts of a life

that once was.

Lifeless breeze lifts

leaves and scrapes

colors around the legs

and across the keys

of a stranded piano.

Dusty and rain-damaged strings —

Toppled bench and scattered chairs —

Motionless windows —

and empty coffee cups

Statues forever frozen in time —

forlorn and with no one to stand still for

Suspended in a concrete ocean of silence —

Neverland

Safe inside this Neverland within me

Where all thoughts and emotions are free

Where no words or actions or

Beliefs are expected of me

Where every drop of rain knows my name

And the forest lets me be me

Safe inside the Neverland within

I can go anywhere,

do anything,

and be anything I want to be.

No adventure unreasonable,

No story too deep

No darkness too dark

In this Neverland in me.

Writing messages in the sands

And carvings in the trees —

Messages no one else will ever read

Here in the Neverland within.

The stars are my friends,

they whisper to me at night.

Never completely alone,

here, *my* story never ends.

— Second star to the right

is where my dreams live on

and exploration, expression,

and reinvention never die —

and are never threatened

in this Neverland within me.

Deep

Numbness suffocates in the deep.

I ask for rope but no one hears —

except for what's "too much" to ask —

Darkness rises and Heaviness sinks

until our Names are One.

Oxygen breaks.

These secrets in mind are too deep to share

— and too deep to keep.

Small bubbles glisten with the whisper of Light.

They keep me alive in the Deep — with just enough breath —

though not enough breath to fight.

Dark water surrounds, black and cold.

My thoughts — written on every undercurrent —

thrash and cut — Oxygen breaks.

I am the Deep — Obsidian Water.

Distant cure, and silent Light —

Up is Left, what's right feels Down.

My voice is the lone, rolling Deep.

Disembodied and numb — refraction

Drift — and sleep.

Prism rays and flecks —

promises of hope.

With it, Oxygen collects.

Lungs afloat, and Courage in hand —

the roaring Deep halts. Light reflects.

Thoughts shattered — and form reclaimed —

The Light and Field breathe gently on my face.

Oxygen mends.

Then slowly —

The Deep breaks

Hands of Poison

These hands have blackened to poison —

they fill the air with toxicity.

Everything I touch rots, festers,

putrefies, then crumbles to dust.

I've lost my healing touch —

without it, I don't know who I am.

And yet with it,

no one would stand by me

with the same amount of love and loyalty.

I used to heal them,

one by one —

and they'd go on their way

without a second thought.

I'd take their troubles,

behind the scenes,

an invisible healer —

endless giver —

and they'd live,

though they'd never really know

how I'd carry —

ghost and guardian —

their troubles behind the scenes,

unseen, and uncredited

for the sacrifices

and the work it took to heal them.

No one returned a kindness.

Always pouring out

and never refilled,

they simply take and run,

deny the needs I present

when I need health,

when I need refilling,

and instead I'm given neglect

and indifference,

and hate,

when all I did was ask.

They turned on me,

and chose to believe twisted

misconceptions about who I am.

A silent guardian, and quiet healer,

someone they'd never

taken the time to truly know.

"Feeble minded and worthless —"

they sent me to public trial with lies,

and never stopped to examine my proof.

I let their harsh words

and assumptions change me —

blacken my heart and hands with pain.

The waters of healing within me

now tainted, they poison me;

and everything I touch dies —

and though my heart for others

hasn't changed,

nothing is the same.

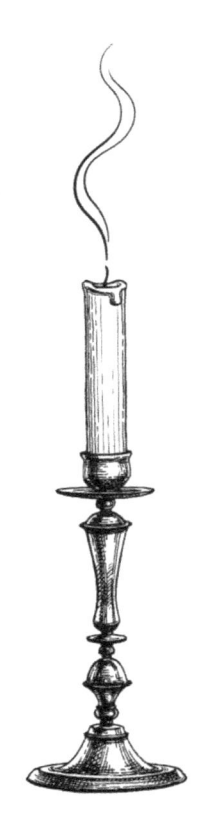

The Dark Ones Made Me

They tried their best

to snuff out my light

make me to be like Them,

and give up the fight.

Their darkness was strong —

it held me captive for years

but now the chains

are made of daisies —

and they can't

hold up against me.

And it hurts to admit —

that They're the ones

who made me.

Because of the pain

They gave me,

I found my freedom —

and courage came to me.

Their doubt and dark lies —

Words of blood —

and Spiritless eyes,

Suffocating grips

of metal hands —

The Dark Ones made me.

They buried me

in barren ground

of ash and past lives —

abandoned.

Deaf to my voice

No one heard me

as the ground swallowed

my cries —

and there in the mud,

with the broken bones

of who They used to be —

just like me —

is where They buried me.

Others They buried

became just like Them

Soulless and resigned —

Damagers of the innocent

creating more of the damned.

But They didn't expect me to rise,

turned toward a new life

Nothing like Theirs —

as They turned Their backs

on me, and left me for dead.

Because of Their broken bones —

I found a way to mend my own.

I found a way to breathe

underground —

and I came out strong.

And it hurts to admit —

that They're the ones

who made me.

Hollow

So empty I cast no shadow

Heavy invisible weight buries

Me underground

Waves overhead deafen

Sound to silence

Where rain is hollow

and mirrors solid —

No reflections to cast back

lightless, haunting faces.

Hollow

Wrapping on doors of my heart

leaves no sound or strength

Rivers of my mind crack and halt

Dust

Where doors crack

and thoughts crumble

Light shines straight

through me

Hollow in ground and touch

Let me guess . . . . I'M the problem?

Stigma

Hate and mental illness,

words without finesse.

For the outside shows no kindness —

all they want to do is "fix" us.

"Mentally ill —"

what they really mean is

"permanently broken."

Defective —

If we dare share our experiences

all they hear is

woe is me, I'm the "victim"

I'm entitled to special treatment

and I'm forever dysfunctional . . .

Because how dare we exist?

How dare we struggle?

How dare we feel

and be human

and wish to be heard

and loved as we are?

How dare we think

and function differently?

But what stigma creators don't realize

is that not all illnesses are permanent —

Most are temporary.

The world thinks it contrary,

but that includes anxiety and depression.

Some may have brain damage

from prolonged trauma, abuse, or genetics,

and some are on the situational

end of the spectrum.

Chronic illness —

temporary battles,

or simple human emotions?

Every emotion is "chronic,"

so why do they dub

the "negative" ones as illness?

They just are,

it's all part of the human experience.

It's simply human to have seasons

of sadness, grief, anxiety, and depression

caused by oppression, maltreatment,

and the situations around us.

The human condition is not confined

to constant happiness

and the false ideal of never being affected

by circumstances and how others treat us.

So why are we punished and labeled defective?

Your dismissal and invalidation only makes it worse.

Oppression can cause seasons to become permanent.

If you never let up or recognize

the damage you do to others,

maybe the trauma you cause us

is part of the problem.

Maybe if there was a lot less

stigma and pointing blame

just to free yourself from

the responsibility

of laying down your pride

for the sake of love and effort,

maybe if there was a bit more kindness

there'd be less *mental illness.*

Medication is not always the solution,

sometimes all it takes

is an apology —

And rectifying a broken history

To improve someone's

mental health.

Providing a safe place of acceptance

and readiness to listen,

and understand —

rather than blaming us,

or silencing us,

and strengthening the stigma

of "mental illness."

Misery Needs Company

Misery needs company —

to be allowed to be human

to be heard —

Not brushed off as

unreasonable

or invalid,

misery has a place.

There is beauty

in sadness

in grief

in silence.

Misery is part of life

and part of the process

— part of healing —

There's something to be said

for needing a friend,

needing to be heard and

understood,

needing to be met

where we are

without expectation

to be "better"

or unaffected by

the storms we find

ourselves in.

We're often expected to

carry our storms alone,

but we were made for

Support, and the need for

love and community through

the storm.

We are not defective

for experiencing a season

of misery.

The season would be shorter

if we simply had

the right company.

To Be Wanted

I want to feel wanted.

I want to mean something to someone,

anyone —

and know they don't

want to go through life

without me in it

instead of casting me away

so easily —

like my presence has

no impact —

on their quality of life.

I want to mean something

and be

wanted —

It seems so easy for people

to give me up

and do without —

There's no pain to cope with

the decision to say goodbye

or that I'm not wanted

like I'm the world's

least favorite ice cream —

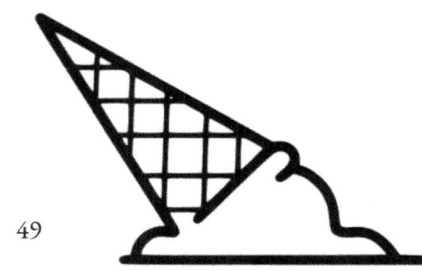

Always in stock

and ready to love,

and be loved,

but always left

to frost over.

A second look

and it's

"No thanks, I'm good."

Like there's no consequence

to leaving me behind.

I want to be wanted.

To be needed

and made space for —

to be accepted

in tenderness

and care

when things get rough

and I make mistakes.

I want to mean something

to someone —

anyone —

and know they'll be there

to catch me

when I can't catch myself

instead of leaving

when I'm suddenly

in a season of

Non-self-sufficiency.

I want to be wanted —

to be someone's

first pick —

and know that

giving me up

would not be

an easy decision.

Or that walking away

isn't an option —

because I'm truly

wanted.

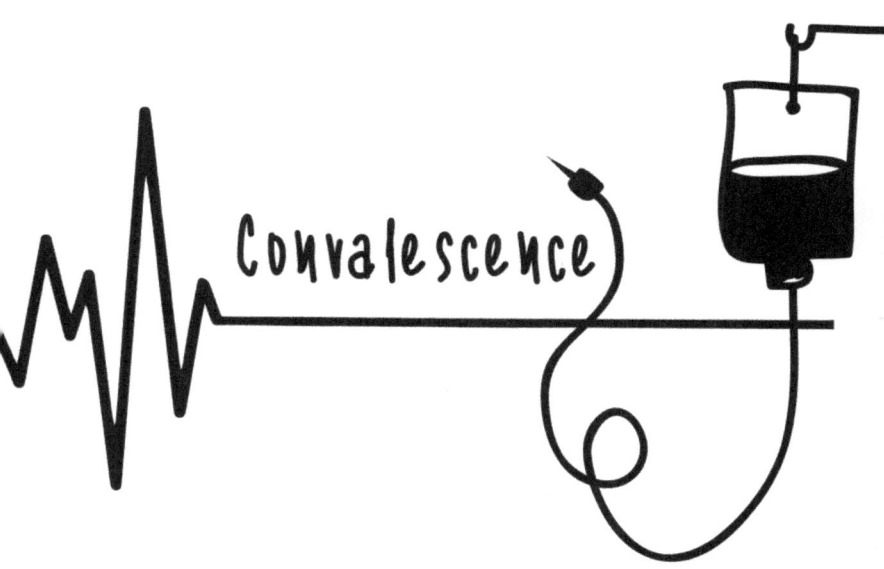

Convalescence

Emergence from darkness is

the hardest fight.

An underrated convalescence

that's strongest at night.

No one else sees you

in your weakest light

when giving up feels like

what's right.

Convalescence, a constant refinement

that happens in silence

and binding confinement.

Growth and healing is my defiance

These wounds and emotions

that cut deep —

realignment

Emotional wounds may as well be physical,

a curved blade through the heart —

exhumation — a miracle

This is my fight,

hidden behind the darkest light —

a convalescence

that creates a battle-strong knight.

This One's For Me

I'm shedding the skin of who I used to be,

the skin others forged and imposed on me.

Created to please and perform,

to hide my true form

and encase me in guilt

regardless of the fight.

So no more choices and actions

for suffocating expectations.

This one's for me.

No more performances

or forced encores for others,

this one's for me.

I choose the new path,

The one I've been taught to ignore,

Because taking the path

Others put me on is a chore,

So this one's for me.

I didn't do this for you,

I didn't do this against you,

This is my life,

And my dream.

This is *my* shot —

So this one's for me.

Your Fangs Are Showing

Soft and agreeable, they think

gentle and kind,

sweet and compassionate,

cute and refined.

They think you're weak,

with no backbone

Until they make you speak.

Until they push you too far —

Triggered, then you stand,

Your smile makes them uneasy

as you take up your power

and speak with passion —

My dear, your fangs are showing —

Your fangs are showing, my dear

you claim your hill

and lift your head with pride,

No one knows you when

you show your fangs.

They want you to go back

to the place you hide —

Their fear tells you to stay

quiet and weak,

and they expect you to agree

But your fangs are showing.

They didn't expect a voice so sound,

You do great things with courage profound,

your fangs are showing, my dear.

Chasing dreams and truth,

breaking the cage —

you smile in your sleep,

My dear, your fangs are showing

Let your fangs show,

don't back down —

you can bring your voice

and show your smile of courage.

Your fangs are showing my dear

My dear, your fangs are showing

Don't push me,

this cinnamon roll has fangs.

You pick yourself up

and your fangs show,

You stand for yourself

and your fangs show.

You speak for your heart,

for your joys and passions

with confidence, and your fangs show

Sometimes silence is wisdom,

but when it is time to smile,

time to laugh,

or time to speak,

it's okay to let your fangs show.

This is my dream.

Has been for years —

Starbursts within

I can no longer contain —

Like piano keys under

Pressure —

My life bursts with sound

This light, I will

no longer dim

for anyone's grim

cynicism.

This is my dream —

Has been for years.

My spirit will no longer

be silent,

and I no longer care

who listens.

People say I've changed,

but the truth is

I've always been this way

I just no longer care who hears me

and I'm not afraid to show it,

because this is my dream —

it has been for years.

Braver By Pen

Spoken words often silenced

breed blank thoughts

— unable to share in confidence —

Spoken words get thrown away

— unheard and lost among the airwaves —

Constantly challenged

— met with cynicism

and the lack of empathy

led me to be

braver by pen than spoken word.

Words that won't come by voice,

or that falter, not by choice,

find strength behind the pen.

Words have weight

written in ink.

They make them slow down

and think.

There's no choice but for them to listen.

So I've become braver by pen

than by spoken word.

With ink,

my voice has a place to go.

I can speak my mind

and take back my soul —

Courage is mine again to be bold.

No more losing my voice

trying to reach those

who aren't tuned to my radio.

It doesn't matter if

they can't hear my frequency

with words written in ink,

because at least I'm seen.

At least I'm read.

Braver by pen than by spoken word,

I can say what I need to

without someone's hand over my mouth.

Because even if they don't accept it,

they can't send back what's been read.

Near You

You watch the world go by,

I find you at the best point of view.

Feathers to wind —

I ground myself at your side

You are rest

But you move further away

Magnetic pull —

I follow

Head on wing,

I want to watch the world with you,

Because near you —

is the best view.

Near you,

a place of comfort.

Together we watch the years go by

But I battle the dying light —

for your attention

and the wind tells you to move.

Let the Raven Mourn

What is this osmium

heavy heart and

mess of obsidian feathers

My raven Soul

has brought me? —

Full of loss

Silent friends

and forgotten self

Forfeit future

Fractured dreams

Rubbled hope.

71

Chaos in the deep

let the raven mourn —

hear its voice

rasping —

rumble and dust

Open the cage —

let the raven mourn

You will feel light again

at the end.

Once We Were Dragons

Once, we were dragons —

nothing in the world

could stop us

We had fire

and powers —

strength of wind,

talon,

and fang

and the blessing

of the universe.

The sky was ours,

the forest our playground —

the sea —

deep adventures unending.

Every star was

within reach

and darkness

couldn't touch us.

But something

clipped our wings —

broke our spirit

and our fangs.

Something

stomped out the fire

so we repressed it

until nothing

seemed possible

and the stars

were no longer visible.

A salamander

chained

to the ground —

Until once again

we found our spark —

And we remembered —

that once —

we were dragons.

Ember Lights

Ember lights on the coastline —

Misty mirrors and gray streets —

Phantom thoughts pull me in deep,

I've become friends with

the apparitions in the fog.

Paper voices in rippling water,

Notes from secret winters.

Ember lights offered —

Tomorrow's current falters.

Golden Hour

Every day

has a golden hour —

no matter what comes

before

or after,

no matter how

dark

or cursed —

a day gets,

twice in a day,

for a moment —

is the gentleness

of golden hour.

So soft

and warm

my spirit

and heart

glow with it.

I lay down my camera

and drink it in —

the time where

suddenly —

everything is okay.

And with the particles

of light

the veil

between life

and magic,

chaos and peace

disappears.

And everything

is light.

You are my golden hour —

the most beautiful light

of all lights.

When I'm with you,

my spirit doesn't bleed,

it breathes —

My heart beats

not with flight

but with ease —

a steady calm

bathed in rays

of golden light.

You pour in

through the shutters

and blinds,

spreading across the house,

covering

the dark walls of my heart —

Golden bands embrace

my spirit

and replace the air

in my lungs —

glow, and deep new breath.

Suspended in golden hour,

Present

with your presence —

no storm

to anticipate.

Let the Trees

Not all trees grow straight —

We're all different.

The choices we make —

Every branch

Every limb

Every bend

Ads to the height —

The reach for life

And unique winds.

Not every root takes

the same path,

grows the same,

or claims the same

pocket of nutrients.

We're all different —

Every bend creates growth

But every one of us

Grows into exactly

What we're supposed to be.

If we keep going,

Strong and tall

With the decisions

that made us,

every bend

in branch,

limb,

root,

and ring —

A forest of individuals

Who fought for a life —

our own.

The one who restricts

or manipulates

the growth of a tree

breaks its limbs.

Find your own

nutrients,

your own

sun,

your own winds.

Your life

and how you grow —

your decisions,

your experiences,

your strengths,

your storms,

don't have to look

like anyone else's expectations.

In the end,

If you keep going,

If you stand through

every storm,

and remember who you are,

You'll become

one among the forest —

A shape of your own.

Torn Sentences

Torn sentences

like words caged

in my throat

and jagged, crumpled pages

that drip ink

and stain the floors.

Torn pages

and scraps

of black scrawled

paper

litter

the dark wooden desk

and windowsill.

Torn sentences

tearing at my chest

and mind —

falling apart

in mid air —

They disintegrate

before they reach you.

And every time

I try to speak

from the forced

silences

you put me through —

tears,

and torn sentences —

are the best

I can do.

Before the Lights
Go Out

Please —

Come home

Before the lights go out

I'm feeling alone —

Waves drift us

so far out

I know now that

you're a seasonal

stay

But I don't want it

that way,

I want you to stay —

So please,

Come home —

Before the lights go out

We're drifting apart —

and I'm waiting for a

Lifeless start

Unconventional — Love

But we're so

far

apart

Ships with torn sails

In a race against time —

The windows grow cold —

I thought I needed

his love in my life,

So I wished he'd come home —

Before the lights

Go out.

But there's frost on the windows again

mist on the horizon,

monsters in my head,

I can't go through this again.

Please —

Stitch up the sails —

he's so

far

out

This fight against the waves —

Tireless race — to stay

I wished to bring back the flame

Before the lights go out.

Seasonal — Love

If there's anything left,

I needed your kind heart here,

but I know different roads

now lead us so far apart.

Please — Love,

Won't you tell me

It's okay

I need to hear you say . . .

I know it's in vain.

The fog rises

and I can no longer see the waves

I cannot hide the pain —

I'm not ready to say goodbye

so please, I wish you'd come home —

Before the lights

go

out.

Unequipped

Unintentional neglect.

No one can hear me,

no one can love me the way I need.

Unequipped —

They're simply unequipped.

Not only do they have

the wrong tools,

but their tools are broken.

Damaged beyond effect,

how can they give me

what they aren't equipped

to give to themselves?

But I'm tired of being alone

Wandering empty roads —

Looking for home.

Every time I find someone —

someone I thought could hear me

understand me —

with complete tools,

tuned to my frequency

the same kind of different —

as me

Something goes wrong and

they leave —

Unequipped

Unequipped to be my friend,

to love me as I am,

not as they think I should be.

So I grow —

On my own.

It's always been that way —

Because my questions are too much for them

My mistakes — too wrong for them.

They're unequipped —

No one will answer me,

or teach me how to grow

and be okay with my humanity.

So I do that for myself —

I find answers myself

And I give them freely to others

And they leave just the same.

So I keep walking this road alone —

looking for answers —

and looking for home —

Navigating by radio

On a frequency all my own —

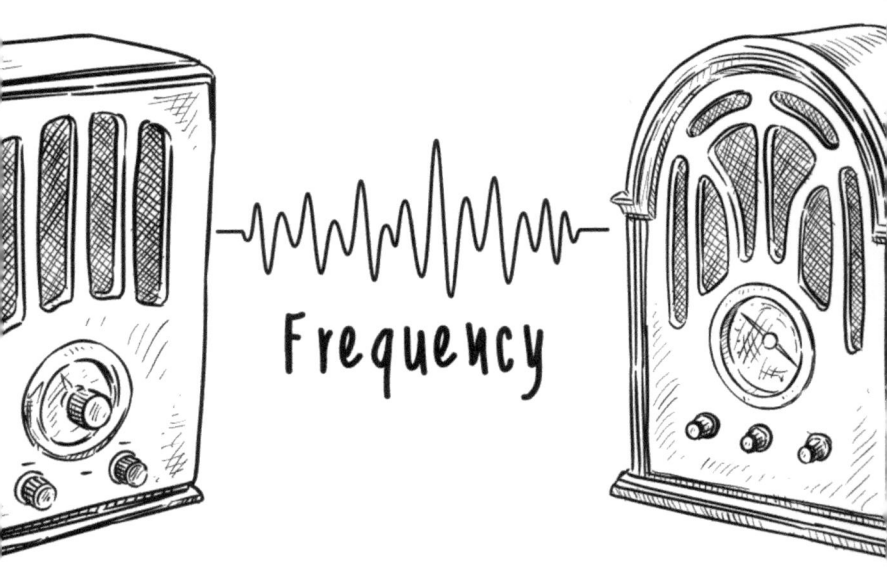

Frequency

Nobody can hear me when I'm in need.

Nobody can hear me when I laugh or speak with passion.

The things I love or need —

it doesn't matter

Because nobody can hear me

on this frequency.

Please, I wish somebody

could tune to my frequency.

Won't anybody hear me?

Can anybody hear me?

My voice is strained —

searching on this frequency.

I'm tired

and hoarse,

my fingertips are numb —

constantly turning dials

and adjusting equipment

as I grow and search,

hoping someone will find me

on this frequency.

But all I hear is static.

Years pass and sometimes

there's a distant voice,

and I try to communicate

but only chaos responds —

it fills the waves and the room.

Some days I feel stranded,

and the static builds

with darkness in my mind

that this matching frequency

will never be found.

But I have hope,

as equipment lights stay on —

no matter how many times they flicker,

someday, I'll find the one

who's also searching for me.

Someone will be on my frequency —

and for the last time,

I'll ask —

Can anyone hear me?

and through the static,

will be a voice full of love

and sincerity to answer —

I'm here.

Broken Ship

Sometimes I feel like a broken ship.

Endlessly striving to fight the tides —

striving for life beyond the horizon.

Growing and obtaining

yet this voyage feels like it's lost

the promise of adventure

and solid ground.

Striving to obtain

new sights,

a new voice,

a new life,

a better direction,

I feel I've lost pieces of myself

along the way.

Lightning cracks

and the angry waves

tear away bits of cargo,

my past —

they gouge the hull, and old self,

snap the mast — break my will,

and shred the sails and my self-belief.

The storm was more than just a storm

that simply required perseverance and growth.

I *divided* myself striving,

and *becoming*.

With no sail to catch the wind,

trying to direct with broken masts

and a jammed rutter.

Striving —

no control over the waves

or my drift,

there's no end in sight,

and no end — I fear

beyond the horizon.

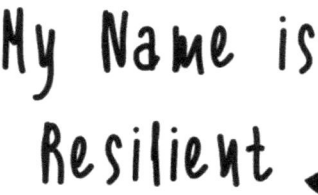

My Name is Resilient

For years, I was resilient in silence.

And now most people see it.

Born to be a fighter I guess,

turning every tragedy,

and every mess

into something that

makes my spirit tenacious.

The will to _live_ and reject the cage —

Determined to break the cycles

and make my own way.

I shatter —

and come back

stronger than before.

Those close to me

often marvel at my courage,

courage they say

they could never have for themselves.

And they call me resilient

every time I grow

and push through the storms.

But maybe my ability

for resilience is simply because

I let myself be shattered.

Every time.

People are afraid to break.

And afraid to accept.

But I'm comfortable

with the shattering

and the darkness —

I believe it's required for growth.

Crucial circumstances

and hostile conditions

build the roots

that ensure you survive

the next storm.

If you let them.

If you let them break you

in the right way.

The kind of break

that leads to the foundation

of reinvention,

and adaptability.

Let the storm

and the break

teach you how

to survive them.

I face the adversity

not with anger or defiance,

denial or strong will,

or stifled emotions and hard work,

but with malleability.

There's no room for

chipped bitterness,

suppression,

or a hardened soul

in resilience.

If you want to withstand

bigger problems,

you have to let them in.

You have to accept the break —

and the emotional wreckage —

acknowledge it,

experience every bit of it.

You can learn from every piece

of the shattering —

every thrash and cut of the torrent,

and not be without the roots or tools

that can only be gained

from the smallest details —

these are the things

you'll need for future circumstances.

Breakage —

it is not destruction.

Breakage is not the end of the story.

Adversity is the lifeforce

for every curve, twist, leaf,

and strength of the vine

that is resilience.

Playlist

There's one for every scene.

And one for every imagination

and emotion.

For the times

you're happy,

peaceful and content —

or bursting with excitement

and joy,

it's the sound of

the electricity

that pulses through you.

For the crisis,

and the crossroad

when you have nowhere

else to turn

but to turn on the playlist

that gets you, and knows your pain

when you're in need of understanding.

Playlist —

universal sounds

for every battle,

every golden hour,

just as versatile as you.

An accessible friend

who always meets you

exactly where you are,

and puts words and music

to the waves it rides with you.

3 am

Awake at 3am —

not full of wandering anxiety

but full of wondering —

Wondering who you are

and when I'll get to meet you.

It's funny how I can miss

someone I've never met

lying awake at 3am —

The sound of a voice I've never heard —

the touch of a gentle hand in mine,

I haven't yet felt —

The scent of your cologne

and pulse of your beating heart

against my face when you hold me in your arms.

I don't even know your name,

but I know you're there,

and one day —

I'll get to meet you outside of my thoughts.

I know I was made for you.

And you're on the same frequency as me.

And I hope that, though I haven't

met you yet —

You're aware of me,

and sending out your thoughts too.

Because even at 3am,

I know I was made for you.

3am —

usually the time when loneliness hits.

The witching hour of darkness or hope —

the strongest anxious, dusty thoughts

of all the things left unsaid, or said unwell —

But sometimes the only thoughts I have

are all for you —

Someone I haven't met yet.

Wondering where you are,

and what we'll do with the future

time we have left.

I wonder who you are

at your core —

What makes your heart beat,

and what makes it bleed.

If you're doing alright

or if you're struggling to survive adversity.

I wonder what you look like,

the color of your eyes,

and your favorite jacket

or hoodie to wear.

I wonder about your favorite song —

the one you connect with the most;

the one that speaks for your soul in ways

you couldn't otherwise express.

I wonder what you're obsessed with,

what makes you tick —

and what you can't live your life without.

I wonder where you've been,

all this time

and where you'd want to go away to

when it's our time —

away to the place that

brings you the most joy,

and the most peace —

the one you can't resist sharing with me.

I wonder what your favorite movie is —

the one that makes you laugh

when you need a reminder of life's amiable qualities.

I wonder what you need

when your heart is sick —

if you turn to your favorite playlist

or watch a show

you've seen a thousand times,

or if you read a book that

meets you where you are.

I wonder what your favorite meal

or snack is —

the one that makes you feel happy

and at home.

And what your spirit needs for rest —

if you prefer silence,

or a creative hobby,

or an afternoon nap.

If you love coffee or tea —

How you take it,

and when we'll get to sit together,

each with our cup

in loving silence or laughter.

I wonder how often you think of me —

because it isn't just at 3am,

I think of you all the time.

And I smile for the day

you're finally in my life.

I often wish that I could message you —

but I don't know your number yet.

And sometimes,

every once in a while —

I smile when I think of you —

because sometimes, it feels like

you're already here.

Messages I Wish I Could Send You

> I love you

> Hope you're doing okay

> I miss you <3

> I saw the cutest cat today!
> Are you sure we can't have just one more?

 Message . . .

What do you want for dinner? I have stuff for curry :)

I found this song and it made me think of you

 ... 2:36

Wanna see something at the historic theater this weekend?

You look really handsome tonight <3

Did I leave my coat in your car?

That book I've been waiting for comes out tomorrow! You wanna go to the bookstore with me to pick it up?

(+) Message . . .

What's your favorite snack for movie night?

Can we go to the coast this weekend?

There's a hermit crab in this tidepool, come look!

Where's the next lighthouse at?

I got your ice cream, where'd you go?

We should get lunch at Mo's :D

THERE'S A NEW JELLYFISH DISPLAY AT THE AQUARIUM!!!

Have you seen my keys anywhere?

We're supposed to be able to see the northern lights at the border after midnight tonight, wanna go!?

 Message . . .

There's a new food truck place, we should check it out!

The Irish bistro downtown is amazing too if you haven't been there yet

[photo of dinner I made]
come over ;)

I wrote 5k words on my novel today!

[that reel I laughed way too hard at, and couldn't stop laughing at for 5 minutes straight.]

I just saw a car honking at an old lady at a cross walk and she hit it with her purse XD

(+) Message . . .

[photo of cats sleeping on my lap]

The cats just stole my bacon T-T and Loki got into my tea

[photo of flowers from my hike]

[photo of waterfall from my hike]

[photo of golden hour light pouring through the trees]

What are you making for dinner tonight? I'm famished ;)

I had a really great evening with you tonight ^_^

Thinking of you <3

Highlights

Life and laughter

like neon lights flicker —

Cozy, misty dark

against soft,

blooming glow.

Amber

and amethyst

highlight the edges

of raindrops and

rippling mirrors

on slate ground.

Highlights —

your hand in mine,

your name on my hair,

and scent in my mind.

Theater lights —

our story written

on the marquee.

Your love in my heart —

highlights — everlasting.

Neon

Her heart flickers —

a dusty neon sign.

Every time she thinks

it's been broken

and lost

one too many times,

It flickers —

and continues on.

XOXO

Consistent color,

persistent strength of light

and everlasting drive

and passion for life —

Producing light

no matter how many ghosts

move into the town around her.

Neon —

her flickering laughter

and glow

always come again

no matter how many skeletons

the ghosts leave behind.

141

No matter how many decades

she's left to flicker on

without another to give her

tender maintenance and care.

She gives enough light

to revive and give hope

to the lifeless bones around her,

but their presence decays just the same.

She's neon —

alone she burns forever

living on her own strength,

finding joy and hope in the small,

infinite elements of Life —

She lives countless lifetimes,

emitting comfort — flickering glow

to dispel what darkness

the ghosts bring her.

City Lights

Raindrops and city lights

decorated the distance between them.

Memories of laughter

now flicker

with silence and broken wishes.

Strength of friendship —

now dark,

left a shadow of melody

as the bright notes

disappeared —

Somewhere —

in the mix of the distant

cool blue,

and ember lights,

is a heart

ready to walk

the next chapter with her.

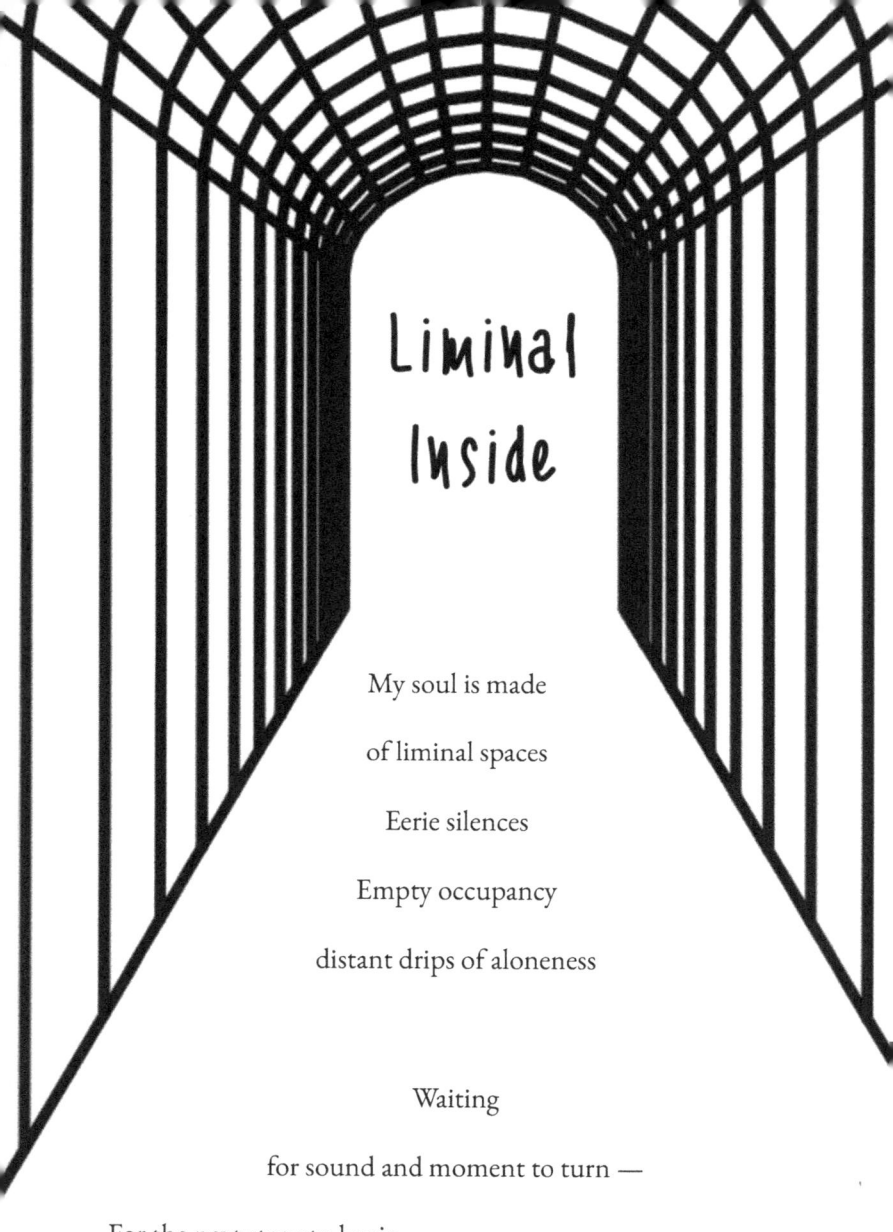

Liminal Inside

My soul is made

of liminal spaces

Eerie silences

Empty occupancy

distant drips of aloneness

Waiting

for sound and moment to turn —

For the next story to begin

I am unfamiliar space

in a familiar face

I haven't even met

the person

I'm to become

Uncertain of what's around the corner —

is it okay to let go?

I walk these empty halls inside

And find hollow room after hollow room

I know them and yet

I know them no longer

How long can I grieve the loss —

the death —

of my past self?

Why does growth have to feel this way?

I can't seem to find her —

the new spirit I desperately

want to step into.

I don't know her,

yet she knows me.

We're the same,

but not the same —

I wish I knew

what it looked like —

This new life,

new hope,

new spirit,

new courage

I'm meant to be.

What do I expect of me?

What does she expect of me?

Empty room after empty room

looking for answers

and the worth I'm supposed to have

in order to <u>be her</u>.

Until finally,

she found me

in the rain kissed field —

she lay next to me

You're still me,

and I will always

be you —

the little girl we once were

will always be part

of everything new.

It's okay to grieve for her,

who we used to be.

Becoming — does not sacrifice justice

for who we used to be,

it brings life and freedom

for who we never *got* to be.

For the woman we always wished to be.

You are her, I am you,

altogether we are still <u>me</u>.

We got to take her further,

the broken girl we used to be,

and we can show her stars

she never got to see.

We don't have to be worthy —

or have finished growing.

All we have to do

is walk through the door

at the end of the liminal hallway —

— the door of becoming —

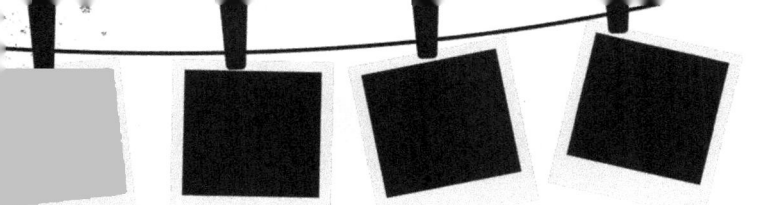

Burn the Memories

They say time heals —

but I don't want

to leave it all up to time —

Amidst the shattered glass —

and memories

the smell of smoke

and crumbling charcoal —

I set fire to the

images in my mind —

153

the scent of you

now fading.

The film's expired —

no more waiting for them to decide

that I'm worthy of their stay.

I'd rather forfeit the past

for the brighter things to come —

Dare to believe that

those I've yet to meet

will cherish me

and the new memories

just as equally —

so I'm not the only one.

I'm too tired

to let the pictures,

cuts and deep scars

fade with time.

So I've decided to say goodbye

to them — all at once.

Memories of false love,

abandonment, betrayal,

after the safety of laughter

and feigned support crumble —

have turned to ash —

hands blackened with soot

and the death of my past —

Blacken the illusion

and burn the loss

to make room for something

steady, healing and true.

I don't want to wait for time

to run its course —

to help me forget

before the seconds move forward again.

I don't want time

and the painful memories

to wreak havoc in an endless loop

of remembering and hoping for better.

I set fire to the memories —

and clear away the ashes,

reduce their power to less —

so they can stop stealing from mine.

Because they say time heals,

but I don't want to leave it all up to time.

For Once

I long to be missed

for once

and told sincerely,

and not be

the only one missing them.

I long to be loved

for once

and not have to always

be the first one to say it.

I long to be cherished

for once,

to be held

and not abandoned

or thrown away

because of my worst days.

I long to be held

for once,

and treated like I matter

and I'm worth their love

even in my mistakes.

I long for love

unconditional

for once,

unwithheld —

even when I'm not at my best

or I do something wrong.

I long for long messages

for once,

that aren't all blue — one sided —

from my end of the screen.

I long to be acknowledged

for once,

for my strengths

rather than my weaknesses —

and celebrated for my gifts

and contributions

instead of beaten down

for the parts of me

that are still in development.

I long to be seen

for my resilience

for once —

and revered for my heart

of empathy and deep emotion

rather than belittled

for what they see

as my "defectiveness"

and innate "wrongness."

I long to be allowed

to get things wrong

for once —

and make mistakes

in my humanness —

and not be treated as less or incompetent

for that one moment I wasn't "right."

I long to be communicated with

for once,

and not be the only one

sharing or trying to mend things

in earnest heart

and vulnerability —

or having to endure being ignored.

I long to be fought for

for once,

and not be the only one

striving for harmony

and health of relationship.

I long to be asked

for once,

to go on real dates

I don't have to plan

or initiate myself.

I long to be heard

for once,

and not have to endure

my needs and heart invalidated —

buried beneath

their pride and narcissism.

Just once,

I long to be loved.

Just once,

I long to belong

and really mean something to someone.

Overdue

I thought you'd

broken my heart

beyond repair.

Apologies are long overdue —

dollars and cents

stacking up —

library fees

I'm painfully

waiting to collect.

You carry on

in apathy —

your indifference

is my entropy.

Nothing affects you,

but my freedom

is long overdue.

Cents and dollars

build up against you

as you use and cast away

what's no longer yours.

But the hurt

accumulates against me —

apologies and freedom

overdue —

I'll never see

the pennies —

they're too little too late

anyway,

mountains of gold —

overdue.

Too much of my life

lost library books —

self, spirit, heart,

and peace,

lent out to your

careless afterthoughts.

I want them back —

I'm building a new life

on the recalled coins overdue.

But I'll cancel the wealth

of debt

and buy back my freedom

myself —

because allowing myself

to close your book

and pick up the next one

is long overdue.

Ink Like Rain

Ink in pen,

bottle,

brush, and page —

Every drop

washes away

the pain —

gives way to the

trapped word —

caged self

like rain on

hallowed ground —

mist in trees —

petrichor on gentle wind,

and diamond flecked

ferns and leaves.

I breathe ink

like the earth breathes rain —

It brings me life,

and solace.

No storm is in vain —

Ink is the canvas

on which my soul

writes,

speaks,

and draws

worlds from within.

Black glistens,

seeping across the page —

taking with it

the words,

emotions,

troubles,

joys,

and dreams

I never get to say.

From every drop,

a new forest grows,

new stars are named —

new seas discovered —

and dusty artifacts are placed.

Liquid obsidian

drips across my heart —

through my veins —

down my face

and from my fingertips.

In the bottle and cartridge

of dusky-raven solution

I found my voice,

restoration and resolution —

it's made of ink and rain —

the effects of which

cannot be erased.

Home Among
the Trees

I found myself

among the trees

— Home —

where I can breathe

in peace

The Shutter

The shutter is a sound of comfort.

An indicator of spirit

grounded in the present.

Dreams sweep through

the trees

with every waft of wind —

I breathe with the rustle

of leaves and limbs —

the shutter clicks

on heartbeats.

175

Peace fills

my lungs —

imagination

fills the lens and frame.

Alone —

just me, and the sound

of nature,

and the crisp, vintage click

of the shutter

at my fingertips.

Lockdown

all the snacks

every night is movie night

write till my fingers fall off

learn to cook more meals

apparently I bake now . . .

cabin fever

waterfall hikes alone

always walk to the mailbox

long video chats and watch parties with friends

4-hour phone calls

spotty wifi — everyone's using it

order delivery for DAYZ

pick up contactless groceries

where's my mask?

read

order more books

pick up 5th unfinished book that week

naps

meditation

buy plants

eat more snacks

video games past 4am

build an island

pray the wildfires don't reach me

start a business

endless research

online classes

take another nap

write more

draw more

create daily

more sleep

research island designs

turnip mania

watch everyone restart their island 10 times

watch the world fall apart online

stay inside, the planet is on fire

catch up on an entire lifetime of things you haven't watched yet

pray humanity heals

pray your loved ones survive

research the vaccine

throw hands for toilet paper

survive the sanitizer-'pocalypse

surprise, inflation

binge all the things

India Ink

I paint my nails black

like they've been perpetually

dipped in ink.

It flows from my heart —

into everything I do

and make.

I wade around

in the bottle —

a dark universe

of endless possibility.

Made of more

than just water

and soot —

from one hand

to the next

new worlds,

but always the same

thoughts —

ink collects

spirit after spirit

and renews them

from bottle to page.

To control ink,

and to be ink —

is the power of water elemental —

but with more substance

and permanence

and similar

refreshment in renewal.

I make friends with

the darkness

and the bottled black sea —

and it helps me grow,

and water, and plant seeds

ever a part of me.

Sometimes I leave the tv on

just to feel like there's another person

in the room —

a friend,

a comforting presence

when I can't sleep,

or while I work.

Sometimes it's just on

to light up the background ambiance

if I don't feel like the sound of music or silence.

I know the characters —

I've watched them live their screen lives

a hundred times,

and listened to their voices a thousand times —

When I call them forth on the tv screen

it's like sitting in the living room with family.

Enjoying their sound and presence

while I do my thing.

As the tv light blooms

and ghostly casts across the room,

even in the dark

it casts directly onto my heart —

and it's like I'm included and known

by the characters I love.

Even though I'm alone,

and the people who play them

have no idea I exist,

they're still a part of my life,

part of the dark nights —

part of the most influential times of my life

and I feel like I'm really not so alone.

Some people don't understand,

they see it as a waste of time,

but on many of the darkest nights —

the tv light was all I had.

And at darker times, having it on,

turned into having it on all the time.

Sometimes I just need the familiarity

of the characters on screen,

the soundtracks,

successes and mishaps

I identify with

and the people in whom I see myself.

Sometimes I imagine they're talking to me,

or we're friends in real life.

Their company isn't just my comfort,

but expressive relief —

as I can live vicariously through them

and pretend their life is also mine,

or that because they made it through

their hard times and mistakes,

I can make it through mine too.

They help me learn,

and inspire my own creativity,

teaching me my craft of storytelling —

plot twists and character development —

Sometimes they give me hope for my future,

and they even say profound things

that implement change.

They're there if I need a laugh,

a change of headspace and mood —

to find inspiration or hope,

or to feel like I'm understood

through the representation in the characters I relate to.

To Be Chosen

I want to know

what it's like

to be chosen.

To be chosen by you —

I'm always the one

choosing others

but others never seem to choose me.

What is it like

to be on the receiving end

of having someone dedicated

to knowing you,

to loving you,

to spending time with you,

to not letting you go

once they have you in their life?

To being chosen

with the same amount

of dedication

in reciprocation

that I love and choose others?

I feel like time,

and time again,

I fall for the moon.

I stack up the books

and the boxes,

the chairs

and the bricks —

anything I can find

in my endless attempts

to reach you.

But the ones I choose

are always out of reach.

Just like the moon.

They touch me with their light

but they're always so far away.

Unavailable —

no matter what I do.

I could become an astronaut

and still

I wouldn't be chosen by you.

So I'm choosing to look

for those who are more grounded.

On the same plane as me —

because maybe then,

someone would choose me too.

Glowing Sincerity

I don't want to be the darkest light —

I fear the cage

and being silenced.

I'd rather live

with someone's absence

than suffer the theft

of my light and confidence.

My sincerity and rawness

makes them uncomfortable —

but I'm friends with my humanity —

and I find beauty in the darkness

that mirrors my light.

The brighter one's light,

the darker, and bigger

their shadows and struggles —

I will not shrink.

I'm not afraid of their size

or the storms they bring —

The messy, raw, bone-shattering

fights make me stronger

and add oil to the lamp

so that light can be brighter —

I don't want to match the smallness

of those around me —

I don't want to dim, or be

among the darkest lights.

I let the shadows come

and magnify my glow —

I bare my rawness

with the sincerity of the moon —

and let myself glow.

If you can't bare it,

then simply don't look.

But don't tell me to hide —

I don't want to be the darkest light.

The Confidence Con

For too long

I wandered unwelcoming corridors

looking for your belief in me.

And all I found was criticism —

feigned support

and the belief that everything I do,

value, and believe

is wrong.

I've been cut one too many times

trying to keep you in my corner

and convince you to see me.

I no longer need you —

nor the belief that will never come.

All you see are my weaknesses

and past mistakes,

you only believe in my worst

even when you say you're giving me

the benefit of the doubt.

There's no hope,

or vision,

or recognition for my growth

and my strengths

and getting you to see them

has become a waste of time.

My voice is lost against the waves.

There's no point

in confiding in you,

or letting you in on the innermost

workings of what I'm building for myself —

because every piece of information

is turned into ammo or blackmail.

So I've decided —

I no longer need you

to believe in me.

I can carry that myself.

I can find someone else

with the strength and vision

to be in my corner —

to believe in me

through all the times,

even when I don't believe in myself.

Because who I need

in my inner circle

are people who are steadfast —

who cheer me on

and can see me succeed

before I've actually succeeded —

when I'm in the process

and I don't have it figured out,

when I'm learning,

at the beginning,

or in the trial and error of the middle.

When I'm exhausted

and can't see the end of the tunnel

and I wonder if I'll ever get there,

or I'm considering giving up.

I need the people who will help me

fight for myself —

when the disappointments come,

when I fall or fail,

when I'm tired,

when the self-doubt takes hold

and the results take longer to show.

I need people who believe in me

when the journey gets hard —

not kick me when I'm down —

or pull me to the ground,

derailing my wins

because they aren't "big enough,"

or the specific milestones you expected to see.

I no longer want

the fleeting support

that leads to empty rooms

in an a cold, empty home

and words of blood drawing knives

of disappointment.

Because convincing me to trust you

and that your voice — full of your own insecurity —

is sound advice,

and then destroying me from the inside —

is the biggest con.

So I bid you goodbye —

I need support

that speaks life into me

instead of bleeding it dry

or feeding me doubt.

Because confidence thieves

don't belong in my corner.

If Only You Knew

If only you knew

how many times

I cried myself to sleep,

or stayed up past 3

because of you.

How many times —

and pieces —

my heart broke into

because of your broken promises

and indifference.

How many times

I forgave you

without a word or complaint

because I loved you —

even when you wouldn't allow me

to speak to you about the pain,

or ask that we mend the rift.

If only you knew

how hard it really was

to earn this strength

and resilience.

The things I made it through

to get here.

Or how many times

I cried in secret

over your absence,

and lasting silence

every time you said

that you loved

how we can pick up right where we left off

no matter how much time had passed

in the gaps

in our friendship.

If only you knew

that I'm not actually popular,

and how many times

I sought out a friend

for connection

and relationship

because no one ever sought me.

If only you knew

the cuts that I've taken

in silence

from the people I love

just to keep the peace

and protect myself

from the further pain

of not being heard.

If only you knew

the cost of my maturity,

the wisdom,

and emotional intelligence,

you marvel at

and what I've been through

to be able to love and give

such kindness

and grace to those around me.

If only you knew

that everything I am

and give to you

comes at a cost.

Sit With Me

No,

I'm not okay.

And I need you

to treat me

like that's okay.

I don't need some weaponized

inspirational quote,

Confucius saying,

cliché colloquialism,

Bible verse,

or positive quip or mantra

from a multi-millionaire —

just sit with me.

Let me breathe —

let me be human —

let me express

that I'm not okay

without trying to fix me

or expecting me

to just snap out of it —

and don't tell me

something's wrong with me

if I can't just turn it off.

Sit with me.

Show me your kindness

and support,

connection,

and presence

are here for me in every season —

not just the good ones.

Show me you'll be

by my side

in the rubble,

not just when we're holding trophies

with a smile.

Help me sort through the piles

when I have the strength to move —

but until then,

sit with me —

just for a moment —

Before I'm expected

to sort through the wreckage

and begin the dusting off.

Sit with me —

in silence

and kindness

and accept

that I'm covered

in dust and sorrow

before you try to make me stand.

Just sit with me

in the moment,

in the heartache,

the anger,

the disappointment,

the instability,

the uncertainty,

the despair —

come alongside me

in the experience

before you tell me

I need to fix it

or pick up the pieces.

Be here with me

to simply listen

and understand —

I need you to make me feel heard

before you speak,

and supported

before you push me

and walk away.

Just sit with me.

That's all I need.

Seeds

For five years

she planted —

in the driest

forsaken ground

every day —

every month

turned into years —

another seed

of hope

and pressing through

the struggle,

the heartbreak,

the internal hemorrhages

and splintered bones —

She sowed more seeds

in hope that someday

things would change.

She'd see the promises

and something — *anything* —

would grow.

Every day

she heard the calling

and could see a future

where the seeds

produced a lush garden —

and everything she'd endured,

everything she'd done,

everything she hoped

and sacrificed for

would present itself.

She learned and grew

each day along the way,

but the seeds stacked up

and still no rain —

no sprouts to gain.

Five years

of planting,

219

of hope,

endless hard work,

and personal growth,

tending to the ground

and nothing to show

but disappointment.

Her hands sank to the earth —

not to plant another seed

but to lay among the seeds

she'd planted alone, through tears,

afraid, fatigued —

and despite the broken bones —

She'd showed up

for five years —

picked herself up every day

even when it felt like she couldn't go on

to plant another seed,

cultivate, and prepare for rain.

But now she can't help but feel

the strength, the courage, the hope

have all left her — they're as desolate

as the seed bed in which she lay.

Through closed, teary eyes

she wished —

if only Elijah could be here

to speak on her behalf

and lend his faith

that the rain would come.

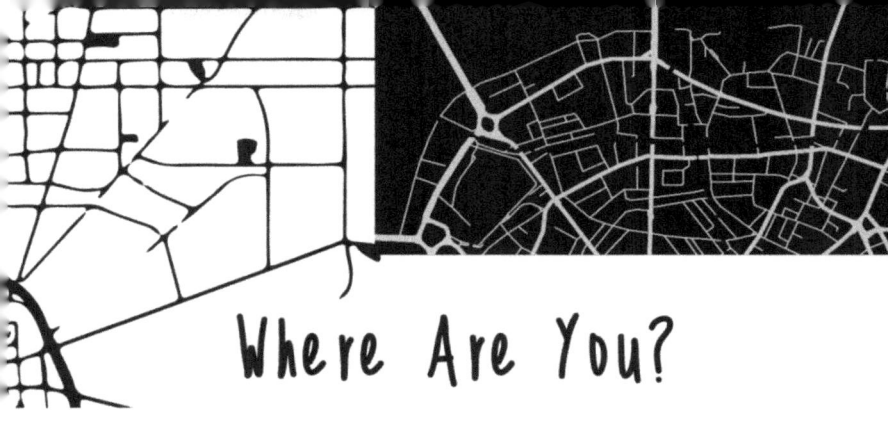

Where Are You?

Author

Hey,
where are you?

I've been trying to find you.

It's just so hard right now
without you.

I wish by now I could have met you.

Everywhere that I look for you —

all I find are dead ends and excuses.

Please,

just tell me —

where are you?

My heart longs

to love

and be loved by you.

Where are you?

I wish I knew

where to find you —

because it's just so hard

right now without you.

I'm just trying to get through

on my own

support

until the day I find you.

I wish I knew where to find you —

Someone to tell my aspirations to,

someone to believe on my behalf

that I can

and *will* reach them.

I wish that I could finally

be somebody

to someone —

maybe it would help me

get through this.

I know you're there — somewhere —

I wish I knew where to find you.

I'm tired of surviving

on my own.

I long for the presence

of a love so deep

it's engraved on his ribs.

Love so true

it makes me forget

all the scams

and disorienting detours

I suffered through

before I found you.

Because

I was born with you

engraved on my heart —

and I'm just finding life so hard

right now without you.

Wake Me Up When It's Over

Wait —

Wake me up

when it's all over —

because it's just

too hard and exhausting

to press through.

I've exceeded

my capacity

for strength

and self-discipline.

I don't want to carry my heart anymore.

Wake me up when it's over,

I want to fall

into a deep sleep

of comfort,

joy,

and peace

knowing that

when I wake up

everything will be okay again —

it's all worked out,

and love is waiting for me —

blessings are waiting for me

when I wake up —

On the other side of the storm.

This torrent has me drenched

and withered down

to the core —

I just want shelter,

and to sleep

through

the rest of the storm.

To sink into the ground

and let it consume

and incubate in silence —

then dig me up

anew

with next month's harvest.

Wake me up when it's over.

Constant growth

and endurance

under breakage

piece by piece

is painful.

My heart longs

for rest

and the storm's end

in peaceful silence.

Sun —

wake me up

when it's over.

This One's For You

You always left me wanting more,

the relationship and closeness

we should have had.

But when I needed help,

you were always there,

so this one's for you.

You lived a life on your own terms.

You called the shots

and worked hard for what you earned.

Like me, you feared the cage,

you told me to make my own way

and I really connected with you that day.

So this one's for you.

With passion — you always did your thing —

and told me to never let anyone

tell me I can't do something.

You never understood the work I'd done,

but you were proud I had my own song to sing,

and that I sang it my way.

So this one's for you.

Fragments

I thought it was all behind me —

I thought I'd fully healed

but you left behind

more fragments than I knew.

I've found pieces of myself

that somehow were hidden in dark places.

I'm still fragmented —

Because of you.

It hurts to see how damaged I'd been,

dusting the cobwebs in the corners of the room —

Digging up ancient artifacts

I thought had weathered away —

And now I have to acknowledge

more pieces of my past

that I just wanted to forget —

to make way for the future I want.

I want to break the contracts

with every lie rooted in my soul —

every pain that found a way

to survive the inner work

through fine print and camouflage.

I want to be whole again —

clear out the back rooms —

no fragment allowed to remain

or secretly keep me from a good life.

Because no matter how much

work I've done,

how far I've come from you,

I find that I'm still fragmented —

because of you.

Borders

Nobody ever talks about

how hard it is

to create healthy borders

and stick to them.

As I lay them down,

brick by brick

and stone by stone,

sometimes crafted

from the very stones

they threw at me

and sometimes the tears

mix with the mud and mortar

I use to past them together.

Borders —

they're for protection,

healing —

and the ultimate test

to see who will respect them

and who will chisel away

at the bricks to pull them apart.

My peace is worth protecting.

My heart is worth protecting.

Even though the ones I love

often cause the most damage.

This is my land,

and no one can cross

unless they've proven themselves

capable and reliable

of taking care of my gardens

instead of destroying them.

Forest Healing

There's something about nature

that's essential

to the healing process.

Physical wounds

or internal wounds —

bring them all to the forest

and the wind,

trees,

and forgiving foliage

lift them toward the sky.

Forest healing —

Nature forces you to take

a deep breath.

To let the sound

of rustling engulf you

as pain and worry

are carried away

as long as you stay.

In nature, I break through

cabin fever,

the weariness from life,

the weight of depression and

emotional wounds

through hikes alone,

park walks,

and photography

excursions.

To touch and smell soft grass,

drifting leaves —

to live among moss,

hear the plants sway

with the breeze

and breathe in the life they give —

to run my fingers through the ferns

in dense trees

near waterfalls

and away from city brash

— a unique elixir

for all of life's ailments.

The Bench

I find myself in a park,

too weary

and numb

to enjoy the wind

and the birds

and the colors

in the trees

or the smell of the air and grass.

I feel I walk

blindly —

searching for rest.

He's there,

on a bench

with the best view,

his presence drawing me in —

At first I can't tell

what he's doing,

but I join him there.

We sit in silence —

and after a moment,

all the pain

transmutes to water in my eyes.

It all pours out

next to him —

on the bench

with the best view;

one I can't even see.

"I'm glad you're here."

It's all he says to me —

As my heart spills out

in endless drops of

hurt and need.

I feel his presence

comfort me —

like the hug I've needed

for years on end.

He gives me

his attention in full,

and listens with grace.

He holds me in his arms

and his words —

the gentle handling

of something precious.

He gives me a minute

and I begin to see.

I ask him what he's doing

as I notice the book in his hand.

"I'm writing your story,"

he says.

"Even as you sit here

with me —

the pen doesn't stop.

My words are always working,

even when you can't see."

He showed me the notebook

filled with illegible writing,

letter after letter appearing

on the pages.

Even as he holds me

in grace and attentiveness —

he's still working on my story.

He showed me the things

from my past,

I saw them in letters I could read

since they've already come and gone —

He directed my eyes

to the view around us

from where we sat.

The bench with the best view —

And the things I hadn't noticed before,

came into focus

as his presence gave me

clarity to see

the provisional trees,

the vitalizing water,

the greenest, softest, comforting grass —

the freshest life-giving air,

and the safety

and provision

in the leaves above my head

and that scattered the ground.

Even here, I don't know

what's to come,

and I still can't read the words

as they appear on the page —

but here,

I can see and feel

peace —

next to him

on the bench

with the best view.

Laurel Triumph

I did it —

though no one believed in me.

They all thought I'd lose it.

Said it was a waste

of my time, skills,

and intelligence.

Nobody saw me.

They threw sticks and stones

as they watched me bleed.

Said I was behind in life already

and I should just give up.

Disappointment —

They said I was smart,

and I was throwing it all away for this.

No one saw the vision.

Selfish, they said —

and I'd never make it.

They said I'd never be successful.

Especially because

I *never have been in the past.*

According to them.

— Where was the evidence? —

they asked.

But now it's here —

and I won the laurel without them.

Despite them —

But I didn't wish to.

I wanted them with me

— to share in the journey —

I never wanted to claim the leaves

or drink the champagne alone.

But some people forfeit the highs

for fear of the lows —

sometimes you just have to go it alone.

With laurel in hand,

at the end —

you have to decide

with whom you'll share the reward.

Should I let them hold the leaves —

and raise them high with me —

whether or not they deserve to?

The wounds they caused me in the thick of it

were great —

when they threw stones as I bled.

To share my win with them —

I'm just not sure that I have that kind of grace.

Sometimes I can't help but feel jaded —

because of the immense hurt

and heartbreak they caused me.

As I struggled to climb through the pit

alone — before reaching the top.

But now that I'm on the other side,

should I also celebrate alone?

Who deserves to carry

these platinum leaves with me?

Those who didn't believe

and now pretend they were with me all along?

Or those I met part way through

and near the end who offered

some small encouragement in the rough.

Everyone wants to take part

in your success —

but no one wants to be there

to make the sacrifices with you

that are required to get it.

For the moment,

I'll just hold the leaves

with a smile

and soak it all in,

this one fact —

I finally made it.

Lantern

I'm letting go of it all —

this past version of myself

there's nothing left

but the words written

on the sides of this paper lantern.

I held on for so long

and fought the completion of change of self

because I felt like if I left her behind —

the one who was broken and harmed

by those she trusted,

I felt like I was doing her an injustice.

But she's safe now,

and it's okay to trade in the hurt

for the love she deserved back then

and seek it for myself now —

to trade in the past

to make space to receive

the next chapter.

So this lantern

is the final goodbye —

and my last wish

to find and live the life

and the love that I always wanted

and that I always deserved.

Because grace will take

the injustice

in exchange for

abundance.

Drifting on black water —

a soft ember glow.

And with the light of a lantern

I send my past untethered —

into the next life.

About the Author

T.W. Glaes is a writer, editor, and a writing and creativity coach. She helps other writers and creatives start creating again, sustain consistency in their creative time, and hone their craft.

She lives in the Pacific Northwest with her two cats. Her works are influenced by her deep love for rain, the trees, symbolism, and vivid imagery. She holds the belief that there is beauty in the darkness and tragedies we all experience within and around us, and in personal refinement, which is reflected in much of her work. She finds inspiration in the many facets that make us authentically human.

Some of the most influential authors who aided her inspiration to write came from her early childhood, and she officially began writing on paper when she was ten. Some of her early influences were Susan Fletcher, Emily Rodda, J.K. Rowling, Avi, Donita K. Paul, Edgar Allen Poe, Keats, C.S. Lewis, and Diana Wynne Jones. To this day, they all hold a special place in her heart.